The Author

Acclaimed as the first artist educator from Japan to teach Japanese brush painting on television since 1957, artist TAKAHIKO MIKAMI continues to foster American-Japanese relations culturally by introducing and teaching Japanese art to more and more American friends.

Born in Tokyo in 1916, his study of art began at the age of nine as an apprentice to his master.

Bestowed many honors and recognized fully in Japan, MIKAMI furthered his career in America with his successful one-man shows held throughout the United States and in Europe. He founded the Japanese Art Center in San Francisco in 1957 and since then, his instruction of painting through television has widely covered the United States, Europe and other countries.

T. Mikami's Sumi Painting

Study of Japanese Brush Painting

By TAKAHIKO MIKAMI.

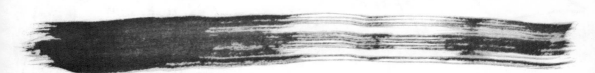

Published by
SHUFUNOTOMO CO., LTD.
TOKYO, JAPAN

Copyright © 1965, by
SHUFUNOTOMO CO., LTD.
19th printing, 1991
Printed in Japan
ISBN4-07-971229-4

Preparation for painting

 **SUZURI**
Grinding stone
water

 **SUMI**
Ink stick

 **FUDE** Brush

A new brush must be rinsed in cold water and pressed out several times to soften it.

SARA Dish

Any white dish as a palette on which to test the tone of SUMI on your brush.

FUDE FUKI
A piece of soft white cotton material to blot excess water or ink from the brush.

FUDE ARAI
A jar can be used for a water well.

KAMI Paper
News print or newspaper is sufficient for practice.

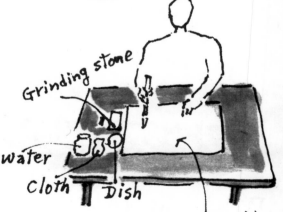
Grinding stone
water
Cloth
Dish
Paper should be placed straight

Japanese SUMI ink is made of vegetable carbon.

How to hold your brush

(A) (B) (C)

Unless otherwise specified, hold brush straight up.

(A) For large strokes, hold brush high.

(B) For small strokes, hold brush low.

(C) For delicate parts, you may use little finger as guide.

How to make shading

(1) Wash brush with clean water.

(2) Blot off excess water with cloth.

(3) Apply dark ink only on the tip of brush.

(4) Hold brush at a slant.

How to prepare different tones

(3) Dilute ink with water to get desired tone.

(1) Make dark ink on SUZURI

(2) Pick up dark ink on brush and apply to dish

Tones

Different tones should be used in a painting.

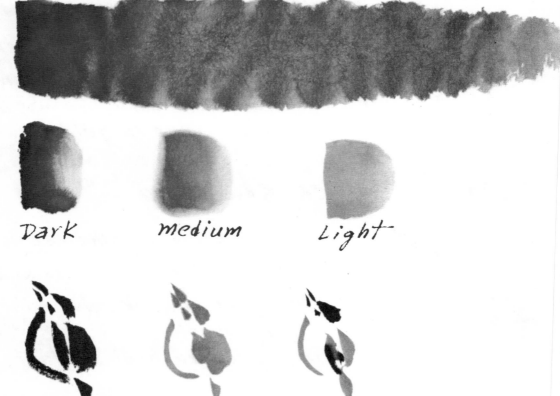

Dark   medium   Light

Dark ink only   medium ink only   Two tones are used.

(Wet brush)

(Dry brush)

Even with the same tone, wet brush and dry brush produce different effects.

— Monotone —
stiff and flat

— Mixed tones —
soft

Arrangement of Tones

This is a combination of three different tones.

Just as rhythm is necessary in music, the rhythm of dark, medium and light is necessary in SUMI painting.

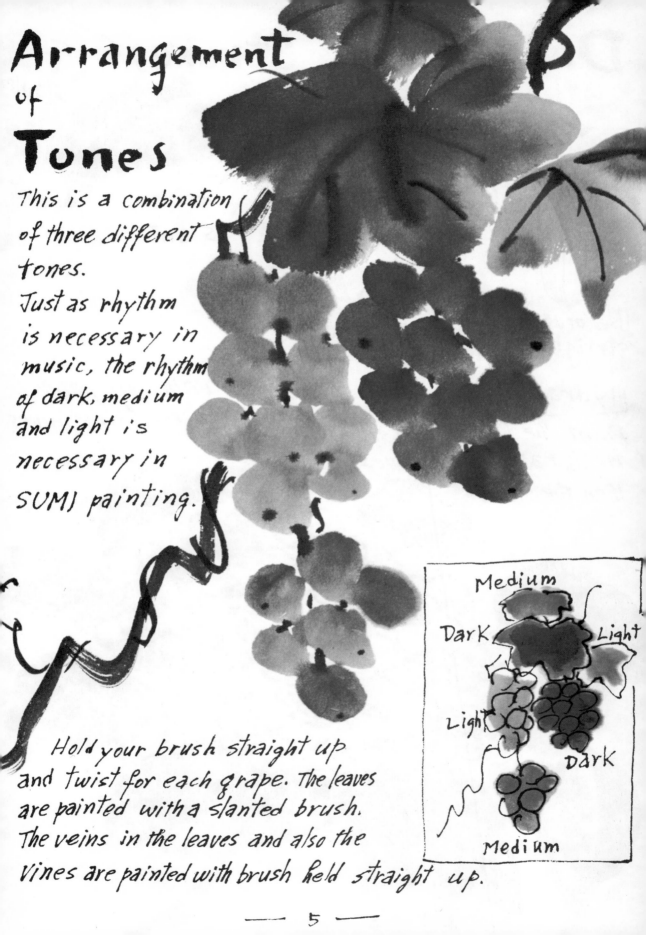

Hold your brush straight up and twist for each grape. The leaves are painted with a slanted brush. The veins in the leaves and also the vines are painted with brush held straight up.

Medium

Dark   Light

Light

Dark

Medium

Dots Lines Strokes

slante[d]

slanted.

Use brush
straight up.

straight up.

Hydrangea

Paint the flower first.
next, paint the leaves,
then the stems.

The veins are painted
on the half-dry leaves.

Two tone combination Japanese Plum

Paint the trunk of the plum with dark ink. Then with medium ink, paint the branches and blossoms.

Accent details with dark ink.

The different stages of the blossom are shown in their order from top down.

Branch

Branch

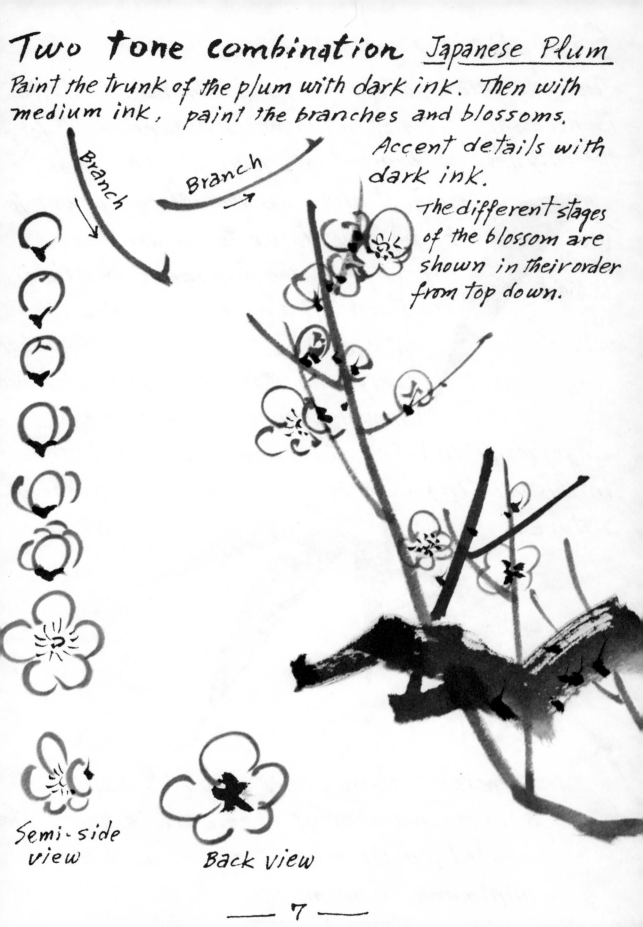

Semi-side view

Back view

Simplicity

Just one small portion of a bamboo branch is all that is necessary for a painting which enables you to forge the busyness of present day living. This small subject alone has the delicate power to bring you closer to nature.

Use brush straight up.

The life of the Japanese and their culture has always been related to nature. Not only this bamboo, but everything that comes into existence through nature can give you enjoyment in life. The five or six leaves in this painting can be said to represent nature.

Therefore, there is no need to paint a large number of them. It is appreciated to produce the highest effect with the minimum in number.

— 8 —

Serenity
Think of yourself as this bird when you paint this scene.

Suggestion of imagination

What is he doing?   What is he
looking at?   What did he notice?

Perhaps his attention was called to
a fellow-pheasant, some other birds, or
falling leaves —— but instead of painting
any of these here,   it is necessary
to arouse the   imagination by
the appearance   of the bird only.

This results
in the
representation
of two subjects
by only one.

order
to
draw.

Pheasant

wing strokes.

spread brush

Expression of feeling

<u>Wild duck</u> Birds and animals looking up at the sky indicate a state of ease or peace of mind. Such subject matter is appropriate for a painting to be hung in a home.

Sketch moving objects first with outlines.
Then practice trying to paint the same
subject in __one stroke.__

Basically these ducks are all the same
and you should be able to paint them
in any position after some practice.

Customs in Japanese painting

As in this painting of the willow branch with the swallow, there are many long established combinations of certain birds with certain trees.

The crane with pine or the sparrow with bamboo are typical examples. This is, however, an old Japanese custom and you need not necessarily follow it.

Make up your own combinations and create American brush painting !

Nightingale

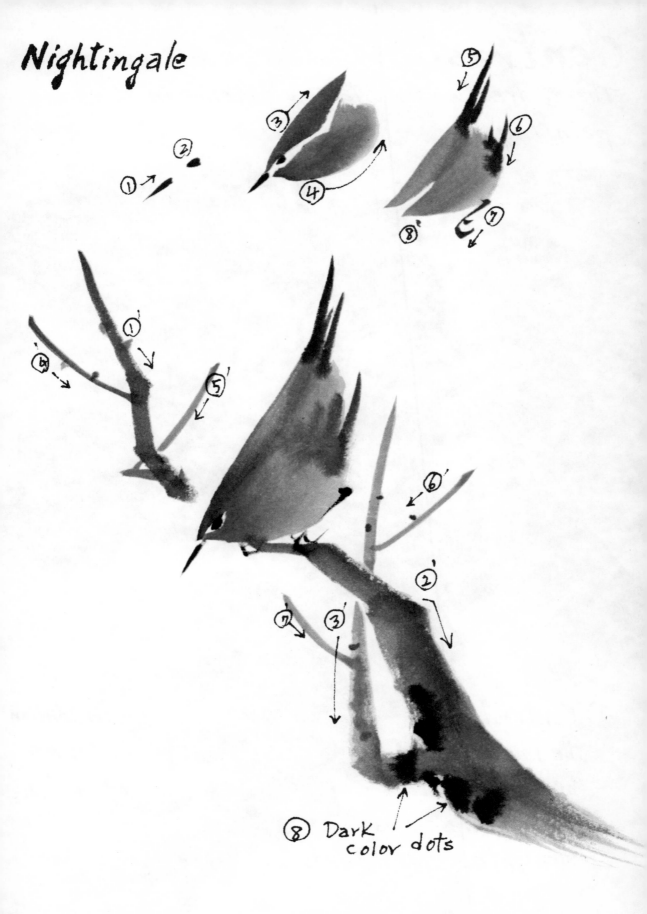

⑧ Dark color dots

Contrast

There are two important elements in this painting.

1) Contrast of
   the roundness of
   the loquats to
   the flatness and
   straightness of the leaves.

2) Gradation
   in tones
   of the leaves

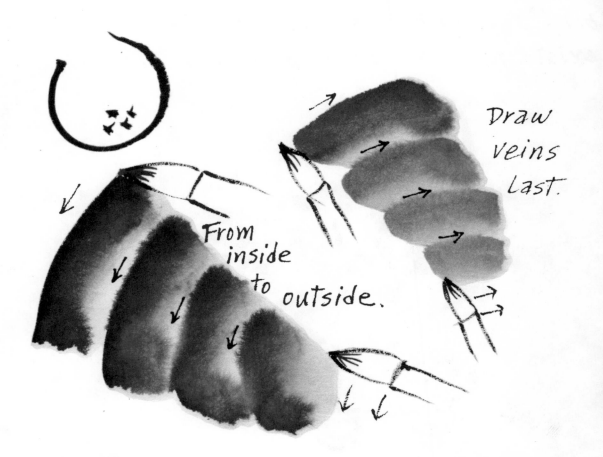

From
inside
to outside.

Draw
veins
last.

Leaves —
vary sizes
and tones.

Spacing

Sparrow and bamboo

By giving him as much negative space as possible, you are permitting the little bird's freedom of movement —— his existence. A bird in a small area

would   be the same as if he were imprisoned. This theory is not limited only to birds.

By painting one of these birds in one corner of a large area, you are giving him the space to fly up or down into.

Leave _above space_ open.

Leave _above space_ open.

Leave _space below_ open.

Simple subjects of Nature

Small objects, often overlooked, become interesting subjects in Japanese art. This is a painting of a bee and a beehive on a branch. Although very small in size, the bee is what makes this painting. It shows movement and life and without it, it would be nothing.

Seasonal subjects

The selection of subject matter determines the season which plays an important part in Japanese painting.

Seemingly unimportant "accessories" may assist greatly in expressing the seasonal aspect — the type of flower, the condition of leaves, certain insects and animals.

It would be an error to place a frog in a snow scene.

Minimum strokes <u>Two chicks</u>

As in various other SUMI paintings, it is desired that
sufficient negative space be left for our subjects
to "walk around" in.

It is appreciated that a painting is completed with
the minimum of strokes.

That each beak has been painted with one line
instead of two is an example of simplification.
Just press your brush to make the body.
<u>Do not go over it.</u>

Practice of small birds

Shaded stroke

No talent is necessary but practice is!
This stroke is used for the fish here,
but you will find it to be very useful
in   many ways. ←

Outlined blossoms
Cherry

For many light colored flowers, a good effect is often obtained by outlining them with light colored ink. However, when painting a white flower on white paper, you can emphasize the existence of the flower by using medium or dark tones for the leaves and calyces.

Petal strokes
Tiger lily

The petal strokes are made by
using the brush flat and
painting vigorously.
Paint from the large
petals first then on to   the smaller.
Each should be done in one stroke.

Deer – Elimination of unnecessary details

Use only the most
necessary lines.
Especially when painting animals
in motion, it is not necessary to
outline the entire.

Rabbit

Dark accent last.

Crab

The crab is a popular subject in Japan — an island country.

In Japan, there are also tiny red crabs living in damp mountain areas. Consequently, Japanese artists often paint red crabs. Do not mistake them to be cooked!

Prawns

In Japanese, lobsters, prawns and shrimps
are written with the characters meaning
"the old of the sea". As many of the old people
of Japan have backs bent with age just as
the prawn, it has long been the symbol
of long life. It is the custom to use
symbolic decorations with
the lobster

at entrance-
ways or in
the TOKONOMA
alcoves of
homes
in
celebrat-
ing the
New Year.

Rose

slanted

① ② ③ center

→

Press

Notice gradation of tones of petals.

Paint petals in center first, working to outer petals.

Leaves are also painted in various tones.

Butterfly

Feelers

Top to
bottom.

Repeat it.

Add dark
ink on top.

Dots and lines are painted over later.

Rooster

The rooster is the symbol for rising early in the morning. Rising early is also a sign of industriousness. As the rooster played an important part in Japanese mythology,

the roosters at the Grand Shrine of Ise are considered sacred.

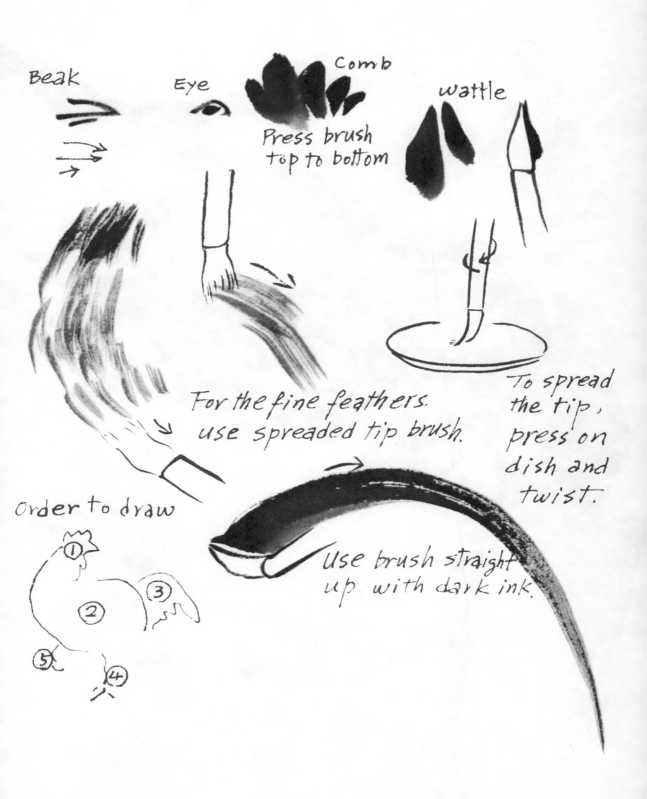

Beak

Eye

Comb

Press brush
top to bottom

Wattle

For the fine feathers.
use spreaded tip brush.

To spread
the tip,
press on
dish and
twist.

Order to draw

① ② ③ ④ ⑤

Use brush straight
up with dark ink.

Horse - A

Head
① → ⑧
⑨
⑩
⑪
⑫
⑬
⑭
— continued →

Horse - B

Line work

This is a SAMURAI warrior of olden times out on a
hunting trip. Painting the subject in this way by
using lines, was also the method in which portraits
used to be painted. These lines are not just outlines,
but must show strength and control of the brush.

Eagle

Paint the beak and eye carefully and steadily, then pait the rest using very vigorous strokes.

Paint the breast feathers by using spreaded brush.

Use your brush flat for the rock with light color ink and add dark ink later.

Human figures

To paint the human figure, you must first comprehend the beauty of lines. This can not be achieved easily. It is necessary to practice thousands of lines. These lines must <u>always</u> be made using the brush straight up. By holding the brush near the top of the bamboo holder, it enables you to use it freely.

Human figures are the subject here but they must not be confused with portrait paintings. It is more important to express *life* itself in the form of a human being,

than to direct all of your efforts towards the resemblance of the subject. It is necessary to practice from many "live models."

Seascape

Example of simplification in a seascape. Gradation in tone from top to bottom in the sail of the boat is the key point in this painting.

Shape of sail can be changed.

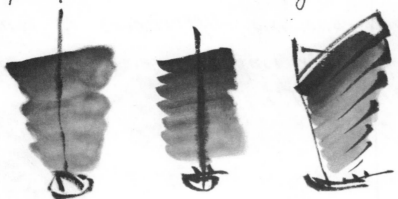

Pine tree
Use slanted brush with dark ink first.
Cover with   light ink   next.

Foreground

(A)

Trunk
from
top
to
bottom.

B

Use dry brush — slanted. (A)

Use more ink for different effect. (B)

Landscape A

The five bamboo, showing differences in tone in the order of their importance, are the main subject in this painting.

Bamboo

Dark color strokes first.
Use brush straight up.

Cover bamboo with
different tone ink.

shaded stroke
with flat brush.

Ground with flat brush.

Background with light tone.
Use flat brush from right
to left — top to bottom.

Landscape B

A typical example of a landscape combining both close and distant scenery. In a landscape, it is necessary to have water in some way as a rule.
This may be, for instance, a river, a waterfall or the ocean.

Example of the composition of a landscape.

Landscape C

This is a common rural scene in Japan. You will find that it is an adaptation of the many different strokes you have already learned.

Landscape D

The darker you make the surrounding area, the whiter the waterfall will stand out.